Rhyme 'n Time™ PHONICS

Word Family Children's Stories

Written by
Larry D. McClellan

Illustrated by
Brian Irwin

Library of Congress Control Number: 2005907518

Manufactured in the United States of America

Illustrated by Brian Irwin
Cover by Krystle Bullard

Art in the Heartland
408 Washington St.
Columbus, IN 47201
812-376-3465

www.artintheheartlandbooks.com
www.im4phonics.com

To contact author:
812-344-0065 or to order 888-884-READ

Larry McClellan has been an elementary teacher for most of his 34 years in teaching. Presently, he is an eighth grade science teacher, however, he's taught from second grade on up through eighth.

Mr. McClellan has always loved children and observed what they have enjoyed reading over those years - like the many animal stories he has focused on in this series. Rhyme'n Time Phonics is only a supplemental reading phonics series for young readers who have already mastered their consonant sounds, blends, etc., and need more help with SOME of the vowel sounds. There are many vowel sounds that we have not yet dealt with in this series, but we have used a majority of them.

Larry has also observed a very beneficial reading strategy that really makes a difference in children's phonics development - namely, word families or word chunking. "Mr. M," as the kids call him, often used word families to teach reading. In the 1970's a study by Wylie and Durrell identified 37 phonograms, showing how over 500 primary grade words can be learned by using word chunking. Larry wants to emphasize this point - that the value of this book is in the vowel family patterns or word chunking patterns that the children learn in this story series. But hopefully, these stories will be enjoyable to read also - even down right funny at times!

The brain is a pattern-seeking organ. For example, it will soon observe that not every "a" or "o" has the same sound. It will observe that there are patterns of sounds where usually open syllables direct one sound and usually closed syllables direct another sound. (i.e., so and go vs. dog and fog) Or, the brain may observe that "r" controlled "a" and "o" vowels direct yet a different sound than either open or closed syllables. (i.e., "tar and chore" vs. "tap and chop") It's true that many phonics rules are "made to be broken," but there ARE patterns that can assist the young reader in decoding sound-symbol relationships. Even though there are MANY dedicated teachers, according to the National Assessment of Educational Progress, two-thirds of American children are less than proficient readers and 30 to 40 percent are "below basic" on that scale of measurement. SOME kids can learn reading just by being read to a lot and have a variety of reading material available; but that's not true for ALL kids! Phonics instruction is very important. Fluency in reading is very important. A child's comprehension will improve when they can focus their attention on contextual clues and not be continually struggling with sounding out the words. Mr. McClellan believes phonemic awareness and the application of decoding skills can accelerate reading progress with proper instruction. Word chunking patterns are part of this process.

In this book you'll find a style that's a very unique combination in this series – of combining word chunking patterns placed in a neat "poetic beat," or a Rhyme'n Time beat. This is true with his whole series of long and short family vowel sound stories, along with additional phonic word clustering sound books. There are three book volumes Larry has produced so far. Mr. McClellan has also made available the additional feature of making these individually interactive "coloring books" for the child upon special request from our website: im4phonics.com. This should help in having the young reader take ownership in the reading process, or just "have fun coloring!" Brian Irwin, a very creative art teacher from Columbus, Indiana, did a fantastic job in providing excellent, stimulating drawings for this series that captured the story's contents in an entertaining way.

Added to these features, the family patterned words are highlighted in bold to assist the novice reader in identifying and decoding the patterned sound. This phonics family focus is available for initial preparation in the list of the "Phonics Family Word List" at the front of each story selection. You may wish to read some or all of this list with your child/student before you read the story itself to them. Larry believes this list to be an invaluable aid to the teacher or parent guiding the child's reading education. Some of the lists also present suffix endings, to further the child's awareness of word parts. Next, you may want to read all of the words as you read the story, except those in bold – the target words. Let the child try to sound those out. Please "point out" that the letter or letter family in bold is always the same sound in this story. Then later, the child may want to attempt some of the other words.

The best way to teach reading with this book is a game teachers call "Popcorn." You read the story and then "stop" where the bold words are. Have the child read the bold word, which is a patterned sound. At first, you will want to coach the child. Subsequently, let the child sound out the word with minimal coaching.

We also provide "extended response" questions at the end of each story to offer experiential discussion/comprehension opportunities for follow-up, along with a short writing opportunity connected to the story theme. The child or student may wish to use the Dolch Sight Word List in the back of this book to help them with spelling. Additionally, try using our "pretest" and "posttest" sheets to assess reading growth, after you practice doing one whole book of "short" vowel sounds, "long" vowel sounds, and miscellaneous word clusters – books one, two and three, respectively.

We hope you and your children will "find the neat beat" enjoyment that results from internalizing the sound patterns learned – in a very "unique" poetic/bold word pattern approach. Thank you - for allowing us to help your child "find the magic in reading."

"This book is dedicated to my wife Debbie-
the wind underneath my wings."

You may wish to let your child color the pictures in this book. Some children will take more ownership in the reading journey by their pride of coloring these stories.

Contents

Jane takes the Cake!

Phonics Word List Long "A" Sound

bake	lane	tame	chase	gape
may	wane	game	snail	cape
day	mane	came	ale	shape
bay	pane	name	male	grape
lay	Jane	shame	pale	scrape
hay	cane	blame	sale	age
say	crane	became	tale	page
way	fade	same	whale	rage
away	wade	tail	cave	cage
stay	jade	hail	save	stage
tray	made	wail	gave	maze
spray	grade	sail	wave	haze
gray	trade	jail	brave	daze
they	ate	nail	grave	days
play	late	pail	rain	blaze
pray	date	mail	rainy	glaze
take	fate	frail	pain	amaze
rake	gate	trail	main	ale
fake	mate	aim	train	pale
make	hate	ace	drain	tale
lake	rate	face	brain	paint
sake	plate	race	plain	painter
snake	slate	base	chain	
cake	skate	case	paid	
wake	bait	lace	raid	
shake	wait	place	laid	
flake	waiter	space	ape	
mistake	eight	trace	tape	

My **name** is **Jane**.
I walk with a **cane**.
My horse is **tame**,
With a pretty, pretty **mane**.

Her **name** is **Kate**.
It was my **fate**
To hurt my leg
When she hit the **gate**!

My horse is **tame**,
But I am **lame**.
Being very, very **BRAVE**,
Is the **name** of the **game**!

FLOUR

I like to **make**
What is **safe** to **bake**,
For my friend **Jake**
Who just loves my **cake**!

Jake came from a **cave**
Out off the **cape**.
He likes bananas.
They **make** him go **ape**!

Jake hates to **rake**
When his back is bare.
I do not care,
But I dare not stare!

I do not **gaze**
When **Jake's** in a **daze**.
I **sail** my boat
In the ocean **wave maze**!

Some **gray days**
There is a **gray haze**.
What I **may** see,
Just would **AMAZE**!

I see a pair of **angels**
Sit upon a **whale**.
The **whale** is **pale**,
With a **pail** on his **tail**!

Jane
takes
the
cake!!

Jane says...

"This **tale** is true!

It's not a **fake**.

If YOU saw it,

Your mouth would **gape**!"

It is fair to **say**?
Make no **mistake**.
When it comes to fibbing,
"Jane **takes** the **cake**!"
(Was **Jane** REALLY "**lame**"?)

If you want a **date**,
To ride **Jane's "Kate,"**
Just send your **mail**,
To the **"Mane" state**!

Address:
I.M.A. Tall Tale Fibber
123 Whopper Avenue
My<u>nose</u>grows, 10 N-C!

P.S. I-M-4-U
R-U-4-Me?
(**Jane's** as silly
as she can be!)

US MAIL

Extended Response

Was Jane's horse and ape real? Why do you think that? Did Jane always tell the truth, or did she make things up that were not true?

What does "imagination" mean? When is it good to have an imagination, and when can it be dangerous?

What is a "fibber"? Would you say that Jane was a fibber? Would you be Jane's friend? Why, or why not?

Have YOU ever fibbed about something? Why is telling the truth important?

Writing

horse	rode	I'd	walk	go	farm	animals
riding	would	mom	dad	woods	saddle	ride
I us	friend	pet	like	give	hay	park

If you had a day to spend with a real horse, where would you go and what would you do?

____

____

____

____

____

____

Daisies in May

Phonics Word List Long "A" vowel sound

bay
bays
lay
lays
pay
pays
may
nay
ray
rays
say
way
ways
lay
laying
pay
paying
play
playing
pray
praying
say
saying
slay
slaying
spray
spraying

staying
sway
swaying
clay
bray
fray
okay
ail
ailing
bail
bails
bailing
fail
fails
failing
hail
hails
hailing
jail
jails
jailing
nail
nails
nailing
pail
rail
rails

railway
snail
tail
tails
tailing
trail
trails
trailing
trailway
wail
wails
wailing
wake
fake
make
maker
making
lake
take
taking
rake
raking
shake
shaking
snake
stake
aid

maid
paid
raid
afraid
gain
gainful
pain
painful
main
mainly
brain
grain
stain
staining
stained
stainable
bade
blade
fade
wade
wading
trade
shade
grade
grading
sail
sailable

plain
plainly
faith
faint
braid
brain
grain
stain
staining
stained
stainable
ace
face
case
chase
lace
pace
place
able
cable
table
fable
gable
label
stable

One **day** in **May**,
I went out to **play**.
"The sky is **gray**,"
my mom would **say**.

"Come in to **play** with your
clay **today**."

I walked like a **snail**
That was **frail** and **pale**.
When it came to smiling,
I guess I would **fail**.

I looked at my **clay**.
I was sort of in **pain**.
I asked myself,
"Was it REALLY going to **rain**?"

There was a **ray** of hope,
Crying would not **pay**.
The sun would bring a **rainbow**,
Then "winks" and says
"**OKAY!**"

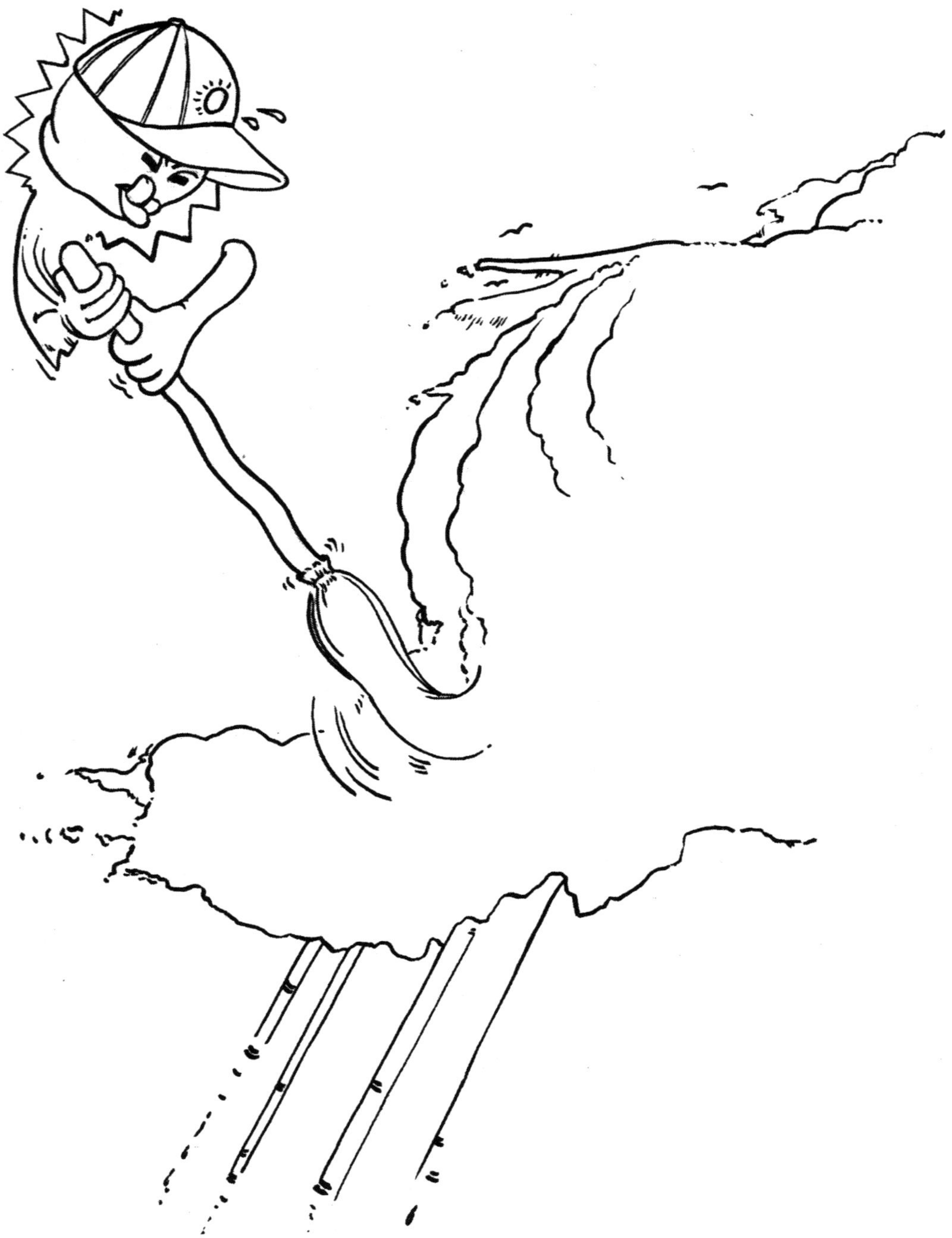

Rain, rain, you go **away,**
Come and **stay** some other **day.**

The **gray** went **away**...
and the blue **laid claim** to the sky.

Soon I said, "**Hey**, **hey**!
The **gray** went **away**.
So now is it **okay**,
To go outside and **play**?
May I PLEASE, I **say**,
Go outside **today**?"

But mom was having a bad **day**.

She began to **wail**,
When the kitty cat's **tail**,
Bumped all of the **mail**,
Right into the **pail**!

Then the cat ran **away**,
Like a **May day stray**,
And left a **trail** of water,
With wet **mail** along the **way**!

Mom said with her head,
"NO **WAY**!"
So I folded my hands – as if to **pray**.
She looked at me with just **plain** love,
Then smiled – I said,
"HOO**RAY**!"

I saw a **pail** on the **hay**,
As I walked out that **May day**,
I heard the **bay** of my pony,
Who **waved** her **tail** to **play**!

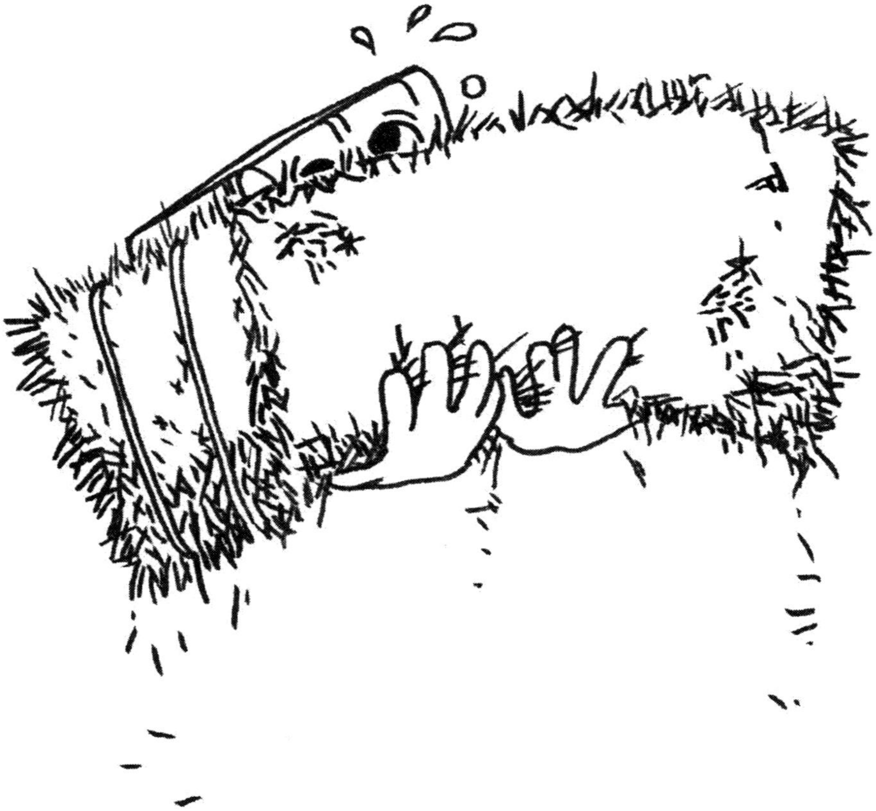

It was no **pain** to my **brain**
When I **gave** my **bay** some **hay**.
She LOVES the yellow **hay**
So she won't run **away**!

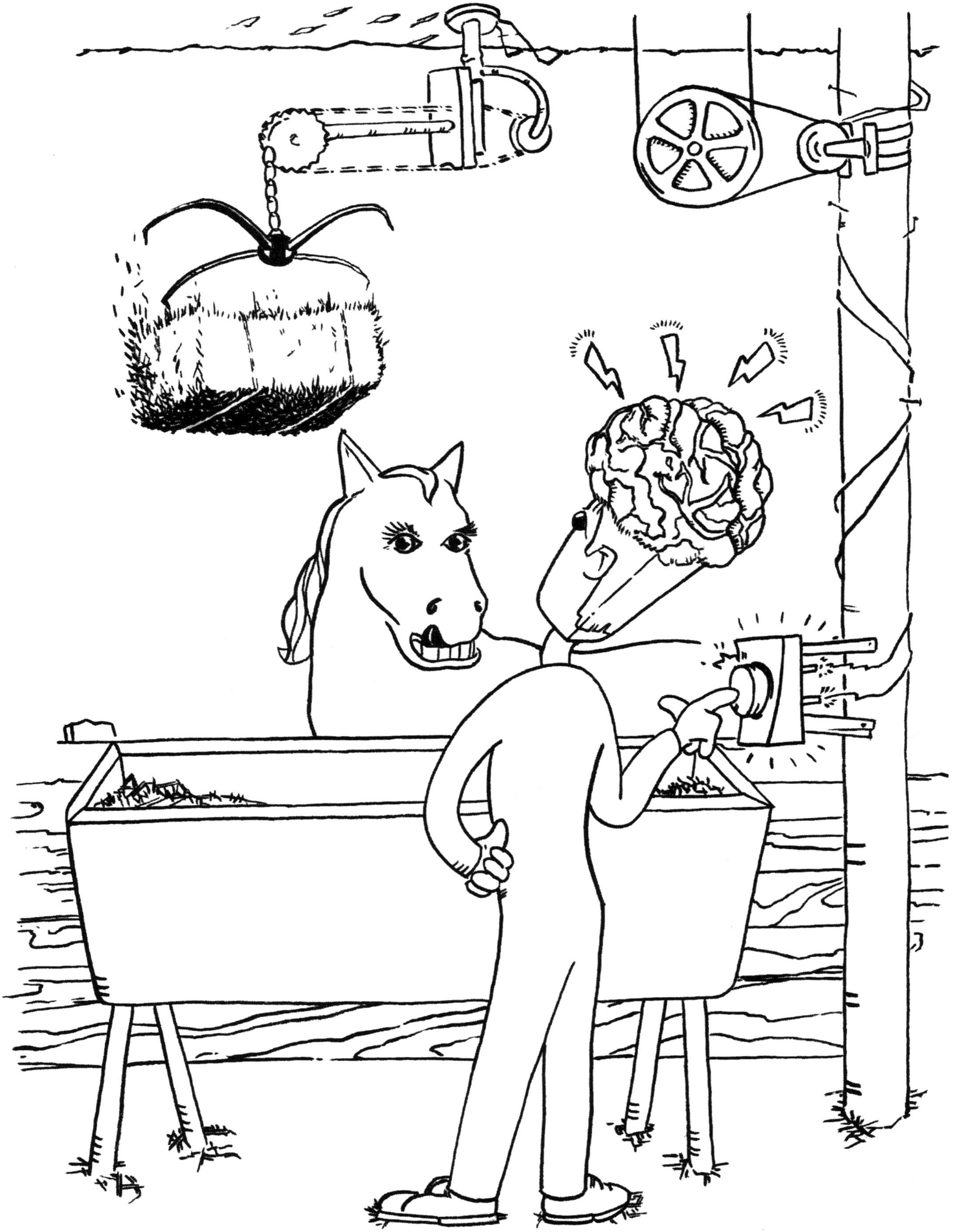

I saw a **train** go by,
On the tracks along the **plain**,
"Tootie, toot, toot
HOORAY FOR THE **DAY**,"
Is what the **train** - seemed to **say**.

Today, **today**, it's time to **play**,
I LOVE to **stay** outside.
Today, **today**, the **daisies** bloom,
They are the sunshine's pride.

(Have a **daisy** of a **day**!!)

Extended Response

Do you think that the boy would rather play outside than inside? Why is that?

Did the little boy listen to his mom when she asked him to do something? How do you know? Are you like that?

What object was resting on the hay? What would you use that object for?

Was the land around his house flat or did it have mountains?

How do you know? How does that compare to where you live?

What kinds of things do you like to do on a sunny day outside?

play	like	toys	I	swing	sandbox	ride	bike
tricycle	jump	merry-go-round	slide	friends			
with	tag	dog	cat	insects	butterflies	clouds	
camping	baseball	basketball	soccer	my	grass		

____

____

____

____

Jean LOVES to Read!

Phonics Word List Long "E" Vowel Sound

he
bee
eat
eats
free
key
me
pea
peas
sea
she
tea
beep
deep
jeep
keep
leap
peep
beat
heat
meat
neat
seat
leads
bead
feed
lead
need
read

weed
seem
team
bean
clean
green
lean
mean
seen
teen
feet
heat
meat
seek
eel
deal
feel
meal
peel
real
seal
steal
heal
keel
reel
any
many
sheet
treat

street
sheep
sleep
sweep
weep
steal
wheel
please
sneeze
trees
cheese
freeze
breeze
keys
bees
ease
these
tease
seem
cream
dream
scream
sneak
speak
week
tweet
wheat
speed
heed

freed
deed
bead
bleed
seed
steed
tweed
icy
ladies
navy
hazy
crazy
baby
babies
silly
story
maybe

Jean just LOVES to **read**,
She is JUST like **me**!
She knows that **reading**,
Is a very "special" **key**!

This "**key**" unlocks many "doors,"
That let **Jean's** mind run **free**.
The doors are really BOOKS you **see**,
Doors to a pretty "storybook" **tree**!

Jean can **read** books with **ease**,
As **she eats** her pizza **cheese**.
But don't **tease Jean** about **cheese**,
LOTS of **cheese** makes her SNEEZE!!

(**Cheese** makes you **sneeze**?
Oh, **please**...)

AH-CHOO!

Some nights **Jean reads** in her **seat**,
Far from the fireplace **heat**.
But near nine or ten o'clock,
Jean winds down counting white **sheep**!

Jean reads about a **real seal**,
That swam **deep** in the hazy **sea**.
A bear came by on an icy **sheet**.
(He thought he found a yummy **treat!**)
The **seal's** heart skipped MORE than a
beat!

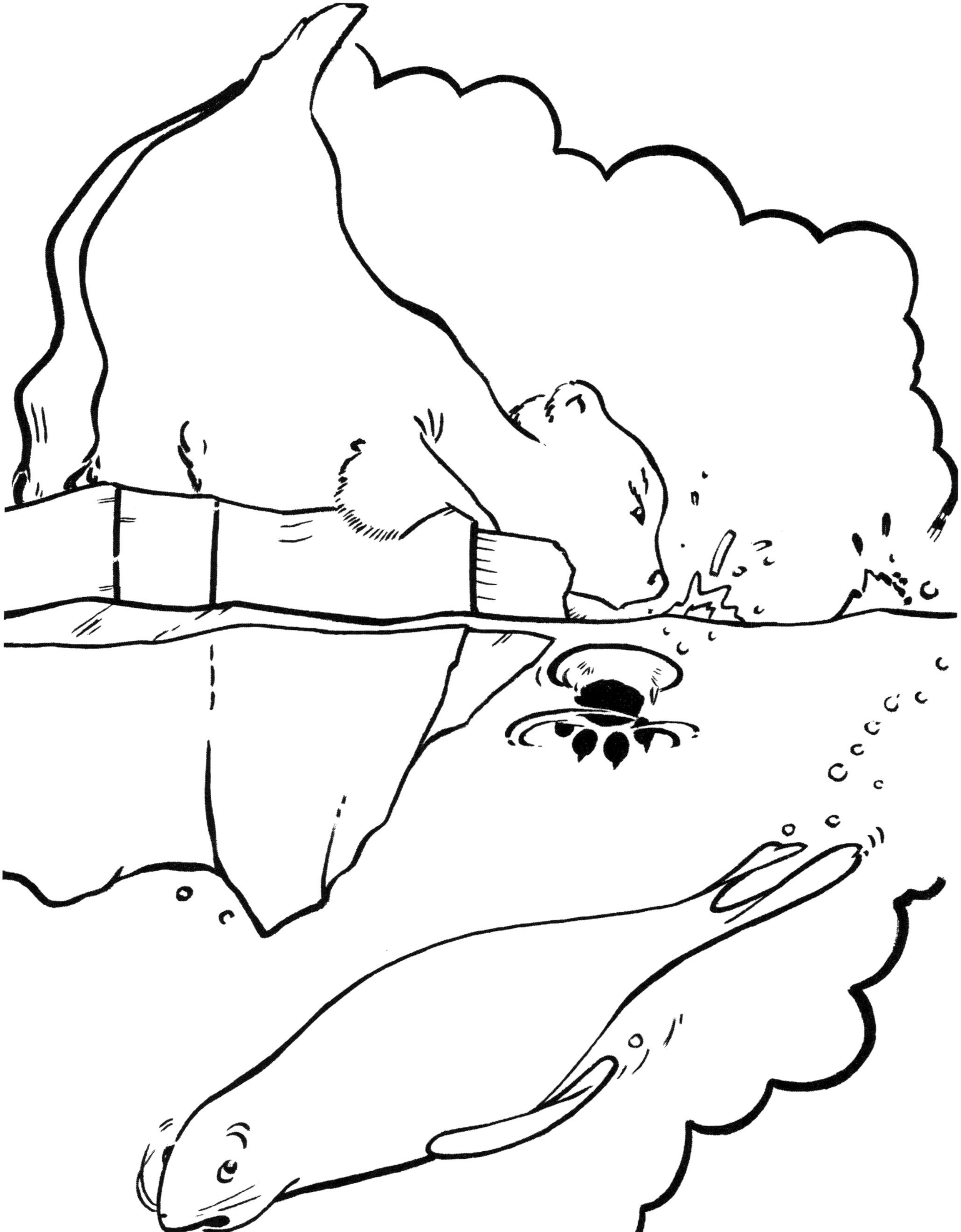

Jean LOVED to **read each** day
of the **week**,
She planted many **seeds** for thought.
Jean would "**steal** away the hours,"
Her "book time" is what **Jean** sought!

ARTS
HISTORY
FICTION

Jean spoke about the story of a
magic **bean**.
A boy named Jack would climb it's stalk-
that looked **pea green**.
He climbed like a fly
right up to the sky,
And found a giant's Boston **cream** pie!
(Yummy yummy in my empty tummy!)

Jean loved a story about a **steed**,
A **lean** horse that wore a coat of
"**tweed**."
He would "**leap**" to his **feet**
with sonic **speed**
And race to do a silly horse **deed!**
(He did it for the **hayseed feed!**)

Jean licks her tasty **ice cream**,
When **she reads** about a soccer **team**,
That **leads** all others in winning scores,
Who go out camping and **eat** S'mores!

I **scream.**
You **scream.**
We all **scream.**
For **ICE CREAM**!

Scream?
For **ice cream**?
That's not too **keen**,
If you know what I **mean**.

Maybe YOU have found **reading**
That very special **key**
That unlocks books with **ease**.
Stories - that take you places,
Like a **leaf** in a summer **breeze**!

Extended Response

Why do you think Jean loves to read? Do you love to read too? Why?

What is a favorite story that YOU have read? Can you tell me about it?

How important do you think reading is to being successful in school?

How important is reading for people when they grow up and have jobs?

Writing

books	I	love	read	to	animal	my
stories	teacher	like	have	big	when	
funny	me	make	laugh	places	go	mommy
are	pictures	become	can	anything	reads	

Mike and Ike and I

Phonics Word List Long "I" vowel sound

by
fly
cry
dry
fry
shy
sly
spy
sky
why
try
eye
July
apply
pie
like
bike
pike
dike
Mike
strike
five
dive
drive
live
I've

fine
dine
wine
pine
file
tie
line
lime
vine
mine
site
kite
spite
white
crime
chime
time
shine
dime
swine
rime
gripe
glide
hide
ride
side

slide
wide
bride
tide
while
pile
file
mile
tile
dice
rice
mice
ice
nice
price
slice
twice
tiny
spiny
icy
bite
right
sight
might
light
blight
bright
slight

crying
trying
lining
dining
mining
biting
biking
biker
rider
wider
deny
reply

Mike - he's my friend.
He is **twice** as **nice** as a
slice of **spice**!
He looks **like** a spy
From the **F.B.I.**

For the **right price**
Mike will play you a game with **dice,**
Or play a game of hockey
with some **time** out on the **ice**!
(P.S. **Mike** LOVES play money!)

Mike likes to **ride** his **bike**
and play along the **dike**.
I **try** to take him with us
when Dad **drives** on down the **pike**.

Mike likes Ike.
They **fly** up in the **sky**!
And when they **fly** back home
they **spy** out key **lime pie**!

I do not know **why**
Mike tries to eat **pie**.
He always gets **pie**
on **Ike's tiny white tie**!

Ike likes to **fight**
all **night** with his **kite**.
He will **try** to **fly** it
with his **shiny**, **bright light**.

I really **like my Mike.**
He makes me **smile** a **mile!**
He tells me funny jokes
while he **glides** through **my file.**

We "**rime**" in **line**.
What's **Mike's** is **mine**.
Some **time** we **dine**
when the **chime** hits **nine**!

Sometimes we **ride**.
Sometimes we **glide**.
Sometimes we **hide**
behind the **wide slide**!

It's a **crime** to **gripe**
how **Mike** blows a **pipe**.
He blows silly bubbles
that land on my **light**!

Mike's tiny motor**bike**
is really "out of **sight**!"
Will he let you **ride** it?
Mike just **might**!

Mike will not **cry**
unless **Ike's kite**
will not take **flight**!
(He gets <u>SO</u> up **tight**!)

Mike is my best friend,
He's **twice** as **nice** as me.
Some**times** I monkey around,
Throwing **rice** on **mice** that flee!

RICE
MICE

Now it's **time** to say good**bye**
and take a **bite** of key **lime pie**.
Have a **fine** and dandy day...
from **Mike** and **Ike** and **I**.

Goodbye!

Extended Response

Mike and Ike like key lime pie. What kind of pie do you like best? If you had just one piece of pie, would you share it?

Did you ever fly a kite like Ike? Where and when? What happened? Do you know what makes things fly?

Mike tells his friends funny jokes. Do you know any funny jokes? Could you tell us one?

Mike doesn't wear a helmet when he rides his bike. Should he? Why? What could happen? Do you wear one?

Mike blows soap bubbles. Did you ever do that? Did you ever blow REALLY big bubbles outside? What happened?

first	then	finally	play	slide	swing	would			
ride	sandbox	teeter-totter	jungle Jim	monkey bars					
climb	go	the	and	we	run	on	jump	spin	eat

What if you went to the playground with Mike and Ike to play on a wide slide? What would you do at the playground?

____

____

Joel and Cozy Rosie

Phonics Word List Long "O" vowel sound

oak	hose	hold	tows
loaf	stone	mold	throws
oat	broke	scold	cozy
boat	choke	sold	nosy
coat	joke	told	bony
goat	poke	bowl	phony
moat	cope	roll	pony
soap	smoke	toll	slow
soak	spoke	troll	poke
toad	stroke	dose	Rosy
road	woke	gross	Joel
roam	pose	bow	
loan	mope	stow	
foam	nope	row	
coach	rope	yolk	
poach	slope	awoke	
roach	scope	grows	
moan	tone	knows	
coal	zone	froze	
goal	alone	mows	
soap	grope	owes	
dome	hope	pros	
home	those	hose	
poem	old	rose	
note	bold	shows	
rote	cold	snows	
vote	fold	woes	
dole	gold	toes	

Joel was a **cowpoke**
And **Rosie** was his **goat**.
They traveled to a far off land,
By **rowing** in a **boat**.

The **boat** was **blown** off course
And landed far from **home**.
They lost their money in the storm
And could not get a **loan**!

Away from **home**
they looked for a **phone**.
They could not find one,
so they started to **roam**.
They took their **load**
on down the **road**,
And came upon a very **nosy toad**.

They **told** their **woes**
To the **nosy toad**,
Who **posed** a crazy question:

"If it **snows** and you **froze**,
Would you lose your **own toes?"**
I really **don't** believe,
That anybody **knows!"**

The **cowpoke** looked at the **goat**,
And they took a little **vote**.
"This **toad** is a **joke**,
He's lost his **hold**,
I think his brain,
Has begun to **mold**!"

Rose was **no dope**.
She **sold** the **toad** some **soap**.
He took a bath in a pond
To **soak** and **croak**- **no joke**!

Down the **stone road** they went.
They saw a **mole** in a **hole**
Who **spoke** with a **scold**.
It was blind and **bold**
With a really bad **cold**.

"I really cannot **cope**,
I caught a **cold** and I **mope**,
I **mope** and **grope** in the dark,
With this **cold** I bark, bark, bark!"

The **goat** had a **coat**
That was very, very worn.
It's pocket was - just a little bit torn,
Rosie gave her **coat** to the **mole**,
(She really was a caring **soul**.)

The **mole** changed its **tone**,
"A **coat** from a **goat**?
How nice can she be?
She gives me her **coat**,
Then tells me, 'It's free!'"

It was free!

Joel said, "Let's **scope** the **slope**,"
Down by the green sea,
For a **bowl** full of berries,
Just for you and for me."

They were very **broke**,
But they met their **goal**,
Their tummies were full,
Of berries from their **bowl**.

Then they found some **gold**,
Along the sandy shore.
I'm **told** they **sold** the **gold**.
Then they found some more!

"Make a **note** dear **goat**,
To find our **row boat**.
This **stroke** of good luck
Will NOT make <u>us</u> **gloat**!

SS ROSIE
!

They found their little **boat**,
And **rowed** it back to the city.
It **almost** did not **float**,
To sink would have been a pity!

They took all their **gold**
And built a sport **dome home.**
They bought a **coat** for the **goat,**
Near a city they called **Nome!**

WELCOME
to NOME

Extended Response

Were Joel and Cozy Rosie good friends? Do you have any good friends? Who are they? How can you tell they are your good friends?

Why did Rosie give the mole her coat? Was she being nice and do you think she was unselfish? Are you unselfish? How do you know?

Joel and Cozy Rosie found a LOT of money! What would YOU do with a LOT of money and why?

Written

money buy I car build house give poor to feed trip swimming pool gifts make bike new friends pet big

If you could do anything you wanted with a LOT of money, what would you do with it? Write a sentence or two!

Smart Art a Poet at Heart

Phonics Word List "R" controlled vowels

tar	churp	for	arm	cord
car	for	pour	barn	snore
bar	fort	door	farm	snored
jar	sort	more	harming	snoring
are	corn	sore	darn	bore
card	born	roar	harp	boring
lard	horn	tore	carp	bored
hard	torn	wore	tarp	
far	worn	your	sharp	
star	shore	core	charm	
scar	store	form	alarm	
cart	score	horn	fur	
tart	snore	fort	burr	
mart	stork	forty	blur	
part	scorn	horse	her	
dart	sworn	lord	purr	
start	thorn	north	were	
smart	acorn	pork	fern	
chart	sir	porch	germ	
barber	stir	torch	term	
carpet	hurd	bark	nurse	
per	nerd	mark	purse	
dirt	herd	dark	purple	
bird	birth	lark	nerve	
gird	flirt	shark	jerk	
girl	shirt	spark	perk	
firm	third	stark	turkey	

Art was **smart**,
And played his **part**,
As a poet,
But would you KNOW IT?

Like a **teacher** in a **car**,
That loved a movie **star**,
Who drove **far** to see **her**,
But got stuck on road **tar**!

In the **tar** was a "**czar**,"
Who drove a crazy **car**.
He gave a tow truck money,
That he saved up in a **jar**.

The **teacher** was really **smart**,
So he rode a nearby **cart**,
While he **drank** lemonade,
That tasted kind of **tart**!

Art says, "Make-believe is what I see!
Silly tales 4-U-N-4-me!"

Like a **lark** in the **park**,
That would **churp** in the **dark**,
Then flew around a tree,
Right into the **bark**!
(That is silly!)

Art would ask you:
"Have you ever heard a **carp**,
Play some music on a **harp**?"

"Have you ever heard a **barber snore**,
Or **bark** in the **dark**, in the
Park, park, park?"

Have you ever seen:
An **alarm** on a **barn** - on a sleepy
horse farm?
Or a **stork** fly a **dart**
Around a shopping **mart?**

MEGAMART

Art really loves to rhyme,
He does it all the time.
It's **part** of his **heart** you see!
But **Art's** as happy as can be - like me.
But **Art's** as happy as can be.

Art's got questions "1-2-3,"
Questions in poems
4-U-N-4-Me!

Like - "Do you see
D-B-N-D-T-P?"

Have you ever seen a **girl**
Take a **swirl** in a **skirt**,
Who tries to **flirt**,
With a boy in a **shirt**?

Would you **gird** a blue **bird**
that was **hurt** in the **dirt**?
Or tell your mom
you had a "red **alert**"?

Can you **purr** like a kitten,
Or **snort** like a **horse**?

Can you **darn** a **worn** sock,
While on a golf **course**?

Are you the "**sort**,"
That's "**short**" in a **sport**,
And can not ever "**score**,"
When you're down the **court**?

Have you ever seen a **farmer**,
Chase a **turkey** on a **shore**?
The **turkey** gobbled **popcorn**,
From a nearby country **store**.

SNACKER
BARREL

Have you seen a **bird** fly north,
Way up high - away from **harm**,
Or heard your **parent** say,
"Three times is a **charm**"?

It's really NOT a **boring chore**,
When **Art** walks
to a BIG book**store**,
And he finds some great **words**,
So **Art** can RHYME some **more**!

LET'S
READ!

Art LOVES to write us rhyme.
He's **SMART** as he can be!
He makes us **sort** of laugh.
Now wouldn't you agree?

Extended Response

Do you like stories that "rhyme?" Can you name any of them? What words can YOU rhyme?

Do you know what fantasy is? Does this story have any examples of fantasy?

What do you think was the silliest part of this story?

When are YOU silly? Do you know any adults that get silly sometimes? Explain.

Did Art make you smile or laugh in this story? What part? What was funny about it?

Writing

car smart star bird for door horn dark your her were nurse far purple blue red he the is are big blew my drove with mother dad today saw I little shut horse

____

____

____

RhymeNtimePhonicsSeries ________________im4phonics.com

Sound/Symbol Word Recognition Assessment

Pretest _____/100______% Date:_________

Posttest _____/100______% Date:_________

Directions: Circle the words the student misses, (or place a check by each word correctly pronounced) then subtract from one hundred and find the percentage. You may wish to allow for "sounding out" the word first, then saying it. Or you may wish to count it ONLY if they say it "right off." However, note this operational definition and keep it the same for both the pretest and the posttest. You may wish to add a tangible or intangible award for celebrating improvement, however, reading words is really its own reward. This test should be administered at the very onset of the program when it is first introduced. Then give it again after going over all of the stories together, with the child, reading each story at least on three different occasions – and reviewing the "Phonics Word List" three or four times as well. Remember that "a child's hearing improves with praise."

Long Vowel Sound Patterns Story Series 1 – 5 (One point for each correctly pronounced word.)					Total the Points Up!
day	play	say	clay	pale	
fail	snail	pain	brain	ray	
pay	stay	gray	laid	claim	
wail	mail	pray	trail	gave	
log	frog	long	clock	talk	
they	rake	make	cake	shake	
eat	key	tea	keep	heat	
meat	bead	seem	teen	deal	
steal	street	wheel	seat	read	
green	baby	tease	sheep	icy	
seal	steal	speed	story	scream	
fever	peach	family	lucky	stream	
fly	nice	spy	right	time	
dike	pie	white	bright	file	
smart	star	jar	park	farm	
for	shirt	word	dirt	sort	
shore	learn	chore	sport	shark	
fool	blue	cool	scoop	spoon	
school	tooth	room	glue	afternoon	
rock	block	cloth	bought	swap	

Dolch Basic Word List

Teachers know that the most frequently used words in books that children read are called the Dolch Basic Word List. Most children learn these words in first or second grade and consequently have a very good foundation for early reading opportunities. These words must be learned as sight words because they cannot always be sounded out easily by the child and do not typically follow decoding rules. You may wish to print these words in upper-lower case manuscript on 3 x 5 inch index cards and review these to mastery with your beginning reader. If you would like to estimate your primary student's reading level, you can get a good "ball-park" level by having the child read all of the words below with you circling the words they cannot pronounce properly. Add up the words they DID know and use this scale:

Number of Words Recognized	**Estimated Reading Level**
Pre-primer	0 - 75
Primer	76 - 120
1st Year	121 - 170
2nd Year	171 - 210
3rd Year	Above 210

a
about
after
again
all
always
am
an
and
any
are
around

as
ask
at
ate
away
be
because
been
before
best
better
big

black
blue
both
bring
brown
but
buy
by
call
came
can
carry

clean
cold
come
could
cut
did
do
does
don't
done
down
draw

drink
eat
eight
every
fall
far
fast
find
first
five
fly
for

found
four
from
full
funny
gave
get
give
go
goes
going
good
got
green
grow
had
has
have
he
help
her
here
him
his
hold
hot
how
hurt
I
if
in
into

is
it
its
jump
just
keep
kind
know
laugh
let
light
like
little
live
long
look
made
make
many
may
me
much
must
my
myself
never
new
no
not
now
of
off

old
on
once
one
only
open
or
our
out
over
own
pick
play
please
pretty
pull
put
ran
read
red
ride
right
round
run
said
saw
say
see
seven
shall
she
show

sing
sit
six
sleep
small
so
some
soon
start
stop
take
tell
ten
thank
that
the
their
them
then
there
these
they
think
this
those
three
to
today
together
too
try
two

under
up
upon
us
use
very
walk
want
warm
was
wash
we
well
went
were
what
when
where
which
white
who
why
will
wish
with
work
would
write
yellow
yes
you
your

Other Stories Available in the Rhyme'n Time Phonics Series

Book One: "Short" Vowel Sound Patterns

Story 1: Short "A"	**Zat the Rat in the Party Hat!**
Story 2: Short "E"	**Ted and the Pesky Hen**
Story 3: Short "I"	**Nip the BIG Pig!**
Story 4: Short "O"	**Bog the Dog**
Story 5: Short "U"	**Sunny the Happy Duck!**

Book Three: "Chunky" Word Family Patterns

Story 12: "-ink" Family	**There's a Mink in My Sink!**
Story 13: "-aw" Family	**A Hawk that Taught**
Story 14: "oo" Family	**I Bloom in June**
Story 15: "-ack" Family	**Jack and Friends Forever**

Story 16: Short "I" Family Patterns "-ick, -ing, and -ill"
Sid went "Click"

*There are not enough small words in the English language to make a poetic story for this vowel sound.